How to Heal Past

Memories with

Archangel Zadkiel

How to forgive and let go of emotional wounds

Café House Publishing *Interlochen/Michigan*

How to Heal Past Memories with

Archangel Zadkiel

How to forgive and let go of emotional wounds

Z.Z. Rae

Other Books by Z.Z. Rae

Click any link below to check out other books by Z.Z. Rae

- Your Voice Your Choice: The Value of Every Woman
- Ties of the Heart: How to recover from Divorce and Breakups (A 12 step-by-step healing process)
- I Want to be a Unicorn (Why Unicorns are Real and You can be One
- The Middle (I've always said "Yes" to your dreams - God)

Angel Guidance Series

- Angel Guidance for Wealth (Abundant Living for Everyone)
- Angel Guidance for Dreams (Your Dreams explained by the Angels)
- Angel Guidance for Inner Healing (Heal your Heart, Soul, and Mind with the Angels)
- Angel Guidance for Creativity (Unlock Your Gift)
- Angel Guidance for Peace (Allow life's burdens to fade)
- Angel Guidance for Joy (Raise your Vibrations)
- Angel Guidance for Energy Healing (Aligning your beliefs with your desires)
- Angel Guidance for Awakening Spiritual Gifts (Uncover your natural ability)

Spiritual Tools

- How to Work with Archangels: (Guidance from archangels for abundance, healing, spiritual wisdom, and more.)
- How to Declutter with Archangel Jophiel (How to Relieve Stress, Anxiety, and Clutter From Your Life)
- How to Work with Archangel Michael (How do I know my life's purpose?)

- How to Find What's Missing with Archangel Chamuel (There's nothing lost in the Kingdom)
- How to Harness the Power of the Moon With Archangel Haniel (What are the four healing cycles of the moon? Moon rituals to heal the soul)
- How to Awaken the New Earth with Archangel Uriel: (How to awaken, ground yourself, develop spiritual gifts, and live from your heart)

Magical Mermaid Messages

- Magical Mermaid Messages on Abundance (How to manifest money with the law of abundance)
- How to Manifest a Soulmate (with a little help from the mermaids)
- How to Manifest a Soulmate Journal (A journal to attract your soulmate)

Writing Program

- How to Write a Book in 12 Easy Steps
- How to Write a Book in 12 Easy Steps Workbook

For the walking wounded

Intro

I write multiple books at the same time, but for some reason Archangel Zadkiel kept calling to me. Every time I'd work on something else, I'd scroll by her name, and I'd feel this pull. I know this sounds strange, but at times the feeling was a color, or how a color would invoke emotion inside of you. I can't quite put into words *what* color pulled me toward writing this book, but it felt gentle.

Archangel Zadkiel has energy like a mother—gentle, nurturing, caring, and full of unconditional love. I see warm swirling light around this beautiful angel, and to me there is no distinct female or male energy. If I had to pick one, I'd lean more on the female side, although in studies I've done they depict Archangel Zadkiel as more of a he.

In the angelic world, they really don't care what you call them. In fact, I had to laugh, because in one book I read, the author said they were all called 'Michael' (or so she'd been told by her guide). I suppose they aren't picky about their names, but names hold energy and power to them.

While embarking on this spiritual journey with me, have an open heart and mind to receive from these beautiful beings of light. There is purpose in each and every one of these books. I know God has placed this gift inside of me to tune into the angelic energy and give them a voice to the world.

This is a season for the angels to speak. We need them now more than ever.

-Z.Z. Rae

Note from the Author

I write what I hear from the divine. Whether it comes from angels, fairies, mermaids, or a divine source. I let their words be authentic. Have an open mind for the archangels to teach you while diving into these messages. Every book I write changes me, and I hope it can bring you healing.

We never worship angels or pray to them, but we can receive help if we are open to it. I believe these angels want to help spread a message of love to everyone who is willing to open their hearts.

-Z.Z. Rae

Chapter 1: Who is Archangel Zadkiel?

Insert from: How to Work With Archangels

Archangel Zadkiel's name means:

Righteousness of God

Archangel Zadkiel (sometimes known as Tzadkiel, Zachiel or Zedkiel), is the angel to call on when you need a comforting touch, abundance, or healing. Zadkiel is known as the gentlest of all the archangels.

When you look into Jewish writings, Zadkiel is the archangel who brings out compassion and forgiveness within ourselves and others. Zadkiel (as Tzadkiel) governs over the fourth, or Chesed, Sephirah on the Tree of Life in the Kabbalah.

The Chesed sphere helps in aiding one to work on unending love and kindness and expressing it on the Earth. Zadkiel is known as one of the seven archangels in the Gnostic beliefs and also in the Pseudo-Dionysius texts. Having the name Zachariel, Zadkiel is recognized as one of the seven cherished archangels by Pope Saint Gregory.

Archangel Zadkiel's Gifts

Angel of Memory

Archangel Zadkiel can help you when you are struggling to remember figures and facts, especially if you are a student.

<u>Healing Painful Memories</u>

If you are struggling to recover from a rough past, call on Archangel Zadkiel for healing. He can spark the remembrance of your true nature and help you walk in forgiveness. If you struggle with feeling like a victim, Zadkiel can help you walk out of that emotion and into a powerful new mindset.

<u>Emotional Healing</u>

When calling on Zadkiel for emotional health, he'll help you refocus from the pain and back toward the joyful moments you have in your life.

Healer of the Mind

If your mental health is rocky, Zadkiel can gently bring you healing. He'll remind you that you are the one responsible for your own source of happiness. If you struggle with depression or different emotional needs, Zadkiel is the one to ask for help. With a dagger, which emanates violet or blue light, Zadkiel will help you cut through those dark cords.

Helps Children

If a child is in need, Zadkiel is eager to help them overcome their problems.

Abundance

If you are struggling in the area of abundance, whether it's in a material way or spiritual way, Zadkiel is a great helper.

Guide for Unique Careers

If you are thinking of going into a unique career such as a Reiki master, aromatherapist, librarian, interpreter, or psychiatrist, call on Zadkiel to help.

Colors:

Sky Blue, Violet, and Deep Indigo Blue

Crystals and Gemstones

Blue Lace Agate, Amethyst, Blue Chalcedony, and Lapis Lazuli

Scents:

Sandalwood, Ylang Ylang, Bergamot, Rosemary, and Nutmeg

Flower:

Violet

Zodiac Sign:

Gemini

Archangel Zadkiel in a Nutshell

- Angel of Memory
- Healing Painful Memories
- Emotional Healing
- Healer of the Mind
- Helps Children
- Abundance
- Guide for Unique Careers

Message from Archangel Zadkiel

Treasure the moments you have now; for they are very precious and unique. Don't fret so much about

14

the past and all its fears and worries; for you are not living in that experience anymore.

Lift your face upward and expect the very best out of each moment you have. Do away with worry; it doesn't serve you anyways. Let go of the fears of the past. They don't serve you either. I am here to help you walk through things and help you let it go. Fear not, little ones, you are watched over by us.

Affirmation to Archangel Zadkiel

"Dear Archangel Zadkiel, thank you for guiding me through my inner healing, helping me find the things I need, and aiding with abundance."

Chapter 2: Comfort

Let's get cozy. Mmm... The feeling of being comfortable is so nice. It feels good when a warm blanket is snuggled up against you or someone's comforting touch is there. This is where I want to start with you, little ones, feeling comfortable with me.

Stretch, relax, and allow the healing energy to flow through your entire body. While you curl up with these words, let them not just be read, let them be felt. I love to help people feel well-being, not just think about it.

Many of you have gone through horrible methods to heal your emotional wounds. Some of you have been poked, prodded, and felt violated in order to heal yourself. This is not the way I work at all. I work through gentleness, kindness, and compassion. I never push, and I promise you, these words will invoke healing, not force it.

I value the soul

For a human, your soul is unique. Unlike us angels, you hold many worlds stuck inside, which many humans are completely unaware of.

I want to express my awe of your beautiful soul. This is how I want you to view it as well. If you don't value it, it's much harder to desire to heal it. Think of a broken valuable you love. When you value it, you have a desire to fix it.

Your soul is precious and valuable. See it that way. I urge you to at least consider my words with this, because we will only go as deep as you allow.

Never force it

Although, we are working on healing your soul, it is not a process to take lightly. Let the soul guide you where it needs to go.

You will know what step to take and when. This is why you were drawn to my words. You are ready to allow healing to begin on a deeper level. I like to lovingly think of myself as the angel digger. I grab a shovel, I ask you where you want to start, and I dig away with kindness.

It's not that this process is always comfortable. When we hit a root, that's grounded in pain, there will be some emotions coming out. This is a good thing. That means we can uproot that issue, and with my gentle pulling, remove the root of the problem, so that you feel the results ripple through your entire life.

Pain is a good thing

I know that doesn't sound right, especially since I just told you I would handle your soul with gentleness. The level of pain is how deep the root runs. There may be bigger levels of hurt from the start, but as it heals, it feels less and less difficult.

Much like the loss of a friendship or relationship. In the beginning, it can be damaging and painful. Overtime, you soon forget about that person, unless there are things to remind you of them daily. The soul healed itself. You moved on.

I work with you in the gentlest way possible. If you have painful memories arise, remember what I said. The bigger the root—the more the pain surfaces.

It's time to shine a light on your beautiful heart. Are you ready to begin?

Affirmation

My soul is beautiful. I am valuable.

Chapter 3: The Light

The light always dispels darkness. Its job is to remove doubt, fear, and anything that's not flowing right. When you step into the light, the shadows flee naturally. The deeper you go into the world of your soul, the more you'll find shadows dispelling.

More and more you'll be drawn to the light, and you'll find tools to help you clean out your inner being. You may even find yourself nitpicking the dust in the corners, because you've uprooted everything else.

This is perfectly fine, but I want to remind you of a few things.

Your soul will guide you to where it needs healed

If you feel a gentle nudge, and a memory surfaces, this is a sign that your soul is ready to let go of a shadowy past. In the soul, there are multiple levels—much like a house. In each level is a room and stored inside are many memories.

For example, let's say you had a turbulent childhood. That is a layer of the house, and inside each room may be a memory that impacted your daily living.

When your soul is ready, it will open the door, so that we can step inside. Most people fear stepping inside alone. That is why I am here to help you sweep out the things that need resolved.

I'm here to help you clean out the old memories.

Your mind will always understand these are your personal memories, but strange enough, we can change them to feel better. We can rewrite them with love and allow healing to flow to these areas.

21

I'm unafraid of sweeping light into the rooms you allow me in. I never override your will. My job is to assist you in cleaning out the memories that have caused you harm. The human soul is like a giant sponge. It absorbs everything and spits out what it absorbs. If we can change what it absorbed, by means of shining a bit of light or truth onto the situation, you'll be shocked what changes happen.

I explain all this first, because I want you to have a solid understanding of how the soul works. Depending on your background, your acceptance level, and your allowance, is how you will receive these words of wisdom.

Let me start off by telling you another thing.

You are not too much to handle

Sometimes when people go into healing mode, they think they have too much pain, baggage, and stuff to deal with. You may think there are far too many issues, which can cause you to close down emotionally from working on any of them. This is what causes souls to be unconscious, and as a result, they simply let their past energy create their world over and over.

Healing is ongoing

While healing is a continuous thing, it shouldn't be a drudgery. It's like a cluttered house. If someone thinks, *this is too much to handle. I don't even want to attempt to clean this up.* Their living quarters would remain the same. Cluttered. Stressful. Low-energy. If not dealt with, it would only build more of the same mess. If they stopped focusing on the entire house, and started in one spot, they'd see their goals accomplished, even if it felt small at first.

The more you clear out, the lighter you'll feel. You'll see light shimmering in the dark corners you thought would never get cleaned.

Where would you like to start?

Affirmation

I open my heart to the light.

Chapter 4: The Divine

The divine is in your corner. Anytime you feel alone, remember you have a team that is on your side. If you've ever felt or thought, *this clutter is too much. I can't deal with it. No one will want to help me with this emotional baggage.*

Well, darling, we do! We are here with our gloves on, our smiles stretched across our faces, and we're ready to take action. I say, *we*, because I'm not the only one who helps in these areas.

You must give us permission to clean out a room—throw something away—and rewrite a memory for the better. Our help only extends as far as you allow. In fact, some of you think you're consenting, but you're really shutting down the help you could receive.

Value your soul

Like I said earlier, you must value your soul's healing to receive from your angelic team who's here to help you. Let's start off with an easy first step.

Ask yourself what you're ready to heal.

Give yourself permission to simply ask your soul, *what are you ready to heal today?* If you feel you need a day of rest, honor what you're sensing. You may see a memory, hear a thought, or get an emotion that rises. Whatever it is, give yourself permission to go ahead.

I want to give you a little meditation practice that can enhance this process to heal things in your soul.

Meditation

Get cozy. Take some deep breaths. Picture a beautiful house. Whatever type of house that fits your personality. Maybe a dream house you've always wanted.

- Where is this house?
- Do you have a garden, are you in the woods, by the beach, or in a city?
- Picture the front door.
- Give yourself permission to go inside your soul-house. What does it feel like?
- Give your spiritual team permission to join you.
- What does the house look like inside?
- Explore a little bit. What types of things are stored in your house?
- What room draws you?
- Is there a sign on the door?

Take it all in. The door may have a sign or markings to let you know what's inside. You may simply sense intuitively what it means. Are you ready to open it?

- Open the door.
- Once inside, how does it feel?
- What does it look like?

- Do you see anyone in there?

While allowing these images, thoughts, feelings, or sounds to come into your mind, start exploring it a bit. We are here to do some emotional work. Whatever the room holds is ready to be resolved, healed, or cleared away.

Allow us angels to assist you in the decluttering.

Rewriting a memory

There are many ways to do this in different cultures, and I'll try to be as simple as possible.

There are two versions of yourself located in this room. One version is the wounded part of your soul, and the other is the healthy part. In shamanism, the healed and damaged soul part goes to a place it feels safe. In this meditation, the house is your safe place (and place of pain too).

You don't have to go far to meet these two sides of yourself. Go up to the wounded fragment and let it talk to you.

- What is it saying?

- What are you seeing?

Permit that side of your soul expression, because it's in this room for a reason.

- Find the healed portion of your soul.

Once you've given your wounded self permission to express, find the healed part of your soul. She/he may be invisible, until you've fully let the wounded side speak. When you find the portion that's healed, lead it to your wounded self.

Let the healed part talk to the wounded fragment. Observe what it's saying. The healed self will show unconditional love to the wounded self. If it's not…it may be another wound.

- Like a sponge, let the healed part receive the wounded self.

  Allow love to flow through this entire exchange. Us angels will aid you through this entire process.

- Do this as much as you feel you want to in this meditation.

30

If you feel led to visit many rooms in one session, feel free. If your physical body seems drained after this encounter, give it rest. Go as fast or slow as you wish. There is no rush with this process.

You may notice that after this encounter, your mind and body seem different. Many times, you will feel both lighter and a bit more drained. This is because, you detoxed a part of your soul. When you detox, the process needs time to adjust.

Drink lots of water. Eat a healthy diet. This will enhance the body adjusting to this process.

Affirmation

I give myself permission to heal.

Chapter 5: Clearing Memories

When it comes to healing past memories or trauma, I like to take it in a little different approach. In the last meditation we talked about how your soul is like a house. It is the space that holds your thoughts, feelings, and experiences. You are not what's in the room itself, but rather the structure that holds everything.

When you identify with the memory as *you,* you'll find it much harder to clear things out. For example: if you were raised in a turbulent household where nothing ever felt safe, you may struggle with relationships feeling hazardous.

Let's take your relationship with your father for an example. If your father was an unsafe figure in your life, yet you longed for love, you may come into contact with many father figures who treat you much the same way. Your room of Father will be full of clutter.

Each time you experience a father-like figure who was unsafe, you will pack him into the same room. If you identify the room as you, it'll be much more challenging to open the door, clean out the memory, and identify with the house itself, instead of the room.

You are always in control of what your soul contains. It may not feel like it, because some memories, emotions, or experiences seem to dominate the house itself. Some memories run amuck through the house and cause all kinds of chaos. If your mind races, your emotions are all over the place, and your memories dominate you, it is time to clear your house.

Let's say you invite a stranger into your home, and this stranger begins to destroy your belongings and ridicule you. Wouldn't you find it quite bizarre to keep that stranger in your home, and let him have his way in there? Or, would you call the police, kick him out, or find another way of taking back your space?

Every memory in your space (your soul or house) is under your control. If you find one memory is causing pain, havoc, and overall destruction, you have every right to call it out, clear it, and protect yourself. This type of cleaning house is essential with negative past memories.

This isn't ignoring past wrongs done to you and allowing people to get away with their bad behaviors.

It's simply taking power back over your soul, and not allowing that person's behavior to control you anymore.

This type of work isn't done overnight, but it starts with an easy first step.

Step 1

You are in control of your space

Similar to the stranger illustration, you have complete control over your internal space. What dominates is up to you. Needless to say, if you've let memories, emotions, and experiences run amuck for years, it will take a bit of an effort to clear. You can't erase what people have done, but you don't have to allow them to control the space you exist in.

Step 2

Clear out the space

When a memory arises, it's time to look at why. Why is this particular thing ruling over you? Are emotions attached to the moment? Have you fully accepted and embraced how you felt from this particular experience with someone?

Often times, in order to clear out your own space, you have to accept the emotions you felt during the memory. Did you feel small? Unworthy? Unloved? Look at those emotions in the face, and allow them to be heard, felt, and expressed. When you do that, you embrace those emotions with the power of love.

Love heals everything.

Step 3

Fill the space with love

Whenever a memory or emotion is dealt with, it needs love. Love dissolves fear, anger, sadness, disappointment, hurt, and anything else that once filled that space inside of you. Whenever you clear out a room, you'll feel a sense of relief.

Break the patterns

No matter who you are, you have patterns that can be good, and patterns that can be negative. When you've allowed a past memory to rule the roost, you will go through seasons when what you cleared out came back. This is simply because the pattern needs addressed.

If you clear out a room, feel the emotion, and receive love in that area, it needs to be maintained. Memories will be sneaky. They will try to find the emotion you carried by weaving it into another experience.

One way to know you are cleared out is to examine how you *feel* about the memory. You may mentally know you felt bad, but how are your emotions reacting? Are you calm? Have you allowed complete expression? If so—it's much easier to rewrite the patterns that arise. Once the same or similar memory pops up, you can examine it for emotion. If it feels cleared, simply tell yourself, *thank you, but that no longer serves me. I cleared you away. I learned that lesson.*

The more you do this, the more the memory simply fades into the background. It's not that it leaves completely, but it no longer takes up mental or emotional space.

Once you can talk about the memory, without an emotional attachment, you know you've done your homework.

Affirmation

I feel my emotions and give them love.

Chapter 6: The Pain in the Past

Here lies a deep issue many of you deal with. There is still pain in the past. Although the past is over and gone, it can contain emotional pain that you still have to process. A lot of people carry their past mistakes into their present moment, and then push it into their future.

Perhaps you went through a traumatic relationship where you were emotionally, physically, and mentally abused in some way. Maybe, you were naive about the individual you got close to, so it devastated your heart.

I want to be gentle but blunt with you about this. Those things you dwell on from the past don't exist. I know that sounds crazy, because you remember them and feel them. Needless to say, they are gone. Forever. The emotional state you carry is the only remaining factor of the pain you experience. If you simply thought about the time you spent with a person, and don't pay attention to it, it has no power, but once you attach emotion, it can control your life.

Dealing with the past is never an easy feat, but it is a monster everyone has to wrestle. Living with regret will destroy hope of today and tomorrow. When you rewind the past movies in your mind again and again and try to fix what's already gone, it will only create chaos.

If a relationship fell apart in your past, think about it in a few different ways.

- If it fell apart, we were not aligned.
- Did I learn a lesson from that situation?
- Can I value them for what they taught me?

When you look at your past experiences, one of the best ways to heal the memory is to accept the lesson from it. You may not have felt worthy of a good relationship. You can work on accepting and loving yourself, so you'll recognize when someone is treating you poorly.

When you go through extreme pain, such as a bad breakup, divorce, or death, it can be hard to examine the evidence without falling into painful emotions.

Never force pain to arise. When it does, deal with the situation it stemmed from. Often times, when you've faced a bad experience, you may find yourself comparing other people and situations to yours.

When you do this, you are adding the negative energy from the past memory to the current situation. While this may seem like the current problem is *just* like the other one, it is a mirror for you to look at the original problem. When you restore the root problem back to love, you'll find the current situation changes form.

For example, Z.Z. had a relationship where she had no voice. She desired children for years, and she kept being denied what she wanted in the relationship. It was one-sided, so that she became quite miserable in it. After that one ended, she attracted someone else who seemed like he was loving, kind, and empowering in all ways, but as time went on, he too was manipulative, controlling, and not letting her have a voice. In fact, it was worse.

After one more relationship much the same, she finally came to the conclusion that she needed to work on her energy. Once she dove into loving herself and valuing her voice, she attracted a much better, stronger, and more loving relationship.

When there is current pain in your past memories, you must examine why you haven't received the lesson from the situation. When you fall into a self-condemning mode, it will never resolve the pain. If you love yourself, examine why you attracted what you did, and pour healing into the memory, you'll find the emotional pain resolving.

It doesn't mean what the person did was okay. All it means is that *you* received your power out of the past.

Affirmation

I receive my lesson from my pain and let go.

Chapter 7: The Deception of the Past

The past likes to play dirty tricks on you. If it can keep you under its thumb, it will control your every decision concerning your present and your future. The past likes to make you think its helping you, when in reality its keeping you stuck in a pattern of defeat.

Let's say you got out of a relationship where your engagement broke off. The pain of losing someone you were close to can deter you from wanting to connect that deeply again. Your past will say, *don't give your heart. It'll only backfire on you. You can't trust anyone.*

While maybe your mind and heart think it's the best way to keep you safe, it is anti-safe for you. When you don't allow love or connection to flow, it stifles your healing and growth. The human condition is about love and connection with one another. It is about oneness, yet realizing you are an individual expression.

You came to Earth to express your personal energy, but you also came to Earth to connect to the oneness of others. If you cannot connect to the oneness, it may cause pain.

New relationships

When you enter into a new relationship, there is excitement. You learn every little thing about the person. There can be sparks galore going off. Soon, it seems, you start to see little flaws that may remind you of past relationships. Here's where the past memories like to deceive you.

Oh no, he's just like my ex...run away!

She's showing the same signs my ex did when she cheated on me.

Attracting someone like your past experience is part of the healing process. I know that sounds strange. How on Earth could attracting a similar partner *heal* you? This is where I want to break it down for you real simple like.

Your reality is the sum total of your beliefs and thoughts. The more beliefs and thoughts you have surrounding a subject, the more you'll find evidence in your world. If you examine the evidence of what you're attracting, you can easily pinpoint as to why you believe what you believe.

Beliefs can be changed

What makes a belief a belief? It's evidence that the thing you believe is true. For example: if you had a cheating ex several times over, you may fall into the belief that all (men/women) are cheaters. From the moment you start activating your energy to attract a partner, people who may cheat will find you. It doesn't mean they will automatically, but the more you feed that energy, the higher the results of cheating will be.

This isn't to condemn yourself with this knowledge, but rather start working on the memories, feelings, and beliefs of the past. Once you can pinpoint them, it's so much easier to work on the thoughts that surround that subject. Let's just say for example your partner is out late one night doing something. They are being extremely secretive about what they are doing. What is the first thing that pops in your mind?

Examine that thought for a minute. You have the power to change it into something positive. While suspicion happens, you can still turn that *cheating* thought into something else. Whether they are cheating or not isn't the case here, but the fact that you are feeding the energy of them cheating on you.

Instead of indulging on the thought of something negative, change the thought. For if you dwell on the one thought, it will automatically follow another thought back to back. This in turn leads to feelings, which then you will display in front of your partner. This causes several things to happen. Your partner then feels untrusted, unworthy, or unloved, and in turn can lead to the fears you have—cheating. Especially if the emotions you display become much more intense.

Maybe your partner was out late visiting a sick friend, or perhaps they needed a night out to be alone. They could have been putting together a secret party for you. There could be a host of reasons why a partner needs a little bit of space.

Of course, I'd advise you to watch patterns in your partner, because you don't want to be unaware of what's going on in your relationship, but keep an open mind.

Affirmation

I can change my beliefs.

Chapter 8: A Feeling

Sometimes the past memory is more of a feeling than an actual memory you see in your mind. You may simply think about a person and a rush of emotions floods you. These are also memories to deal with, even if you don't have images to match the emotion you are experiencing.

When you go through an emotion, you can examine why it exists surrounding a certain person, timeframe, or event you don't really remember.

Often times, guilt is associated with these types of past memories, because the image of the memory is faded. Let's just say you know something happened at a certain age that caused you anxiety or depression.

You don't even know what that event was, so whenever you experience those emotions, you may feel a sense of guilt.

You may think there needs to be a *reason* for that emotion to linger there, and there is a reason. Whenever an emotion surrounds something—a belief resides. Let's say you have a feeling surrounding a certain relative. Every time you are around them you feel anxious. You may have no distinct memories of anything happening between you and that relative, but your emotions and body do. Trust that.

Ask your emotions and body how you can better serve them. Listen to yourself. If you feel uncomfortable, there is a reason for it. Your feelings are there as a guidance system for you.

One of the most powerful ways to heal your emotions are simply to listen to them. Emotions are indicators of what is going on in your inner world. If you are experiencing depression, shine a light inward as to what is going on. In order for emotions to process, they must be felt, heard, and expressed.

There are many ways to express your emotions, so they can process. There are traditional ways such as talking to a counselor, teacher, or friend. While this often can help, it may feed the emotion rather than express it. In order for it to be expressed, you must let it surface and be felt. If you feel it, it will then dissolve.

The mistake I often see humans making is drudging up the emotions from the past, but not letting them be fully felt. If you feel your emotion is not valid, it may result in expressing without feeling. A sense of guilt may hover over the situation, so the full emotion isn't being felt.

Emotions may feel scary

In your society, emotions are deemed scary. You may see someone expressing how they feel, and one of the first instincts is to run the other way. This is often triggered by a sense of your own emotions that need expressed. If you're not ready for that expression, you may find yourself repelled by others intensity.

If you are a person who feels emotions deeply, this can also be a challenge. Take a few deep breaths, draw yourself into your own emotional space, and be a hand to help them.

You do not have to feel what they feel. You can simply be a guide, a listening ear, helper, or friend for their situation they are going through.

Affirmation

I listen to my emotions.

Chapter 9: What Lords Over You?

Many times, an emotion or past experience will lord over you. The more power you give the past memory, the more it will continue to rule your life. When you look at it for what it is—a lesson you went through—you can apply the lesson and move forward. If you are non-stop rehashing old decisions, it becomes near impossible to receive the lesson. If you haven't processed it, you will keep relearning that particular lesson.

Think of it in these terms. If you had a king, you would be under his constant laws. Whatever he said— was what went, or you'd sorely face the consequences.

If you have a certain time, memory, emotion, or person who rules over you—you would have to follow the laws of that past experience.

If you understand that those past experiences were never meant to lord over you, it frees you to look at them for what they are.

Ask yourself these questions:

- What is lording over me?
- Where do I feel controlled or out of control?
- Is a past memory repeating in different ways?

Once you're aware of these things, next time something pops up, you can ask yourself, *is this a past experience or memory controlling me?*

Many times, humans are unaware of their past repeating. They think it is *normal,* so they don't question why they keep falling into the same patterns again and again. Instead of asking themselves if a specific memory is holding them captive, they find a way to judge the current situation or person.

This just creates a stronger memory associated with the original memory.

I'm sure you're curious to ask: *how do I pull myself out of the past memories?*

Let's dive right into this. Ready?

Let's say you have a past memory of bad relationships. You've had far too many to remember, and the more you have, the more it builds the belief that you will never have a good one.

What if instead of thinking about all those crazy exes, you simply thought about today. Anytime your mind drifted to a past relationship, you gently remind it that the lesson was learned, and you're not living back then. Living today trains your mind to establish new patterns of thought. The more you do that, the more new situations unfold before you.

Let's just say for example in a past experience you ate five chocolate donuts. When you woke up, you immediately thought about those donuts you had, and you felt guilt about eating so many. Throughout the day, you'd bash yourself for being so unhealthy, so that you ended up eating more donuts, chips, and cookies. Maybe you are trying to be healthier, but your past keeps popping up, so you eat to smother the emotions you feel.

Pretty soon, your one experience has turned into today's experience, and it happens all over again tomorrow. Do you see where I am going with this? Don't let your donut-eating experience ruin your today. If your mind drifts to guilty emotions about how you were yesterday, remind yourself, *that was a valuable lesson I learned. I learned that eating five donuts every day makes me feel bad.* Once you receive the lesson from that experience, you can then apply it today, and move forward.

This doesn't mean your mind won't drift to feeling guilty again about consuming those donuts, but you can give yourself compassion from the past experiences. Our lovely author here, Z.Z., always thinks, *that was where I was at emotionally, spiritually, and physically.*

The more you learn, the more lessons you put into practice. When you don't know something—you don't know something. You don't beat yourself up for not knowing the lesson you now put into practice.

This would be similar to chastising a kid for not knowing his A-B-C's—when he hasn't been taught yet. When past memories arise, show them compassion. Show them love. After that, remind yourself that you learned that lesson, and pull yourself into the experience you're having today.

Momentum in relationships

I want to address something, because it can be quite discouraging to some. At times, you've already put yourself into the middle of a situation that can be rather hard to pull yourself out of. Let's say, you married someone who reflected your past experiences and memories of beliefs.

The more you've worked on yourself, your current relationship doesn't seem to line up with what you're moving forward into. This is a tricky thing to overcome for many, because they think, *once I'm committed, I'm stuck here.* I know this is not an easy task, and I know it can lead to a lot of pain, but I want to encourage you in this situation.

A relationship carries momentum. You may have been with someone for 20 plus years, and you suddenly have a wakeup call that you've treated them poorly, or they treated you poorly. At times you are blind to your own faults or the faults of another. The more you start working on your past memories, you'll start to have a clearer eye.

When momentum is rolling in a relationship—it can be difficult to stop it. You've invested energy, time, emotion and past experiences into that person, and if you suddenly change it—you'll experience some backlash. Let's just say you were the jerk in this scenario, and your significant other decided they want to leave you. The wake up was that you weren't always very nice, or whatever the case was, it happened.

Now that you understand how badly you treated your partner—you start to change. Here's where it's painful and difficult for many. Momentum is already rolling, and not to say it can't be stopped, but that partner has years of memories rolling around in their energy. It can be down-right impossible to create the new energy for them to stay.

This can also be flipped. Let's say you suddenly had a wakeup call that your partner has treated you poorly for years and years. The more you grasp it, the angrier you get. When you get this wakeup call, you may start to go against the momentum that's been built, which can lead to many things. It may lead to depression—if you don't make a change, or it could lead to outright hatred.

If you put all the blame on your partner, this brings out a lot of anger, pain, blame, shame, and a host of other emotions that can accumulate. Here is where I want to teach you.

You kept yourself there.

That lesson in itself is a hard pill to swallow. You may walk away with deep feelings of regret, guilt, anger, and a host of other stuff, because in all reality every person makes the choices for themselves—even if it feels like another did it for them.

Your partner didn't force you—you chose that path.

Why?

Well, that's where you were at. That was the experience you expected in your life, and as a result you finally concluded that it was a poor-fitting relationship, and you wanted to move on. That doesn't make you a bad person for moving forward after you received a new perspective.

Here's the kicker. Once you make a tough choice such as leaving, it's up to you to live in today, and not repeat the past again with someone new. If you have a tough time leading your own life, you will attract a partner again and again who will control your choices.

Creating new momentum in your relationship will always be a process, but trust the expansion of what you're receiving.

Affirmation

I receive my lessons and grow from them.

63

Chapter 10: Emotions are Your Guidance

Many times, people think their emotions are a bad guy. They look at them as something to be smothered, controlled, or ignored. They deem certain emotions as 'bad', and other emotions as 'good.' This is where memories can get full of negativity, because certain emotions were never acknowledged or processed through the body.

Have you ever had a certain pain that didn't seem to go away? Ask yourself a few questions.

- When did this pain start to develop?
- What was going on at the time?
- Is there any unprocessed thoughts, emotions, or memories that I'm harboring?

Often times, a painful or frustrating experience triggers an emotion that causes a physical reaction in the body. If you don't pay attention to the emotion, then the body picks it up, and it starts to give you cues as to what you thought, felt, or experienced. The more you ignore that situation, the more the body will react.

The body and the soul are always 100% linked up. There is nothing you do, say, or experience where the body doesn't experience it with you. You're not three separate beings. You are three in one. Body, soul, and spirit. The body picks up trauma, just as much as the mind and spirit.

The body and emotions are a guide

Whenever you fight against the body or emotions, you are fighting against your natural in-bred guidance system. Those two systems will give you clues as to what your energy is currently focused on.

If your past keeps surfacing, and you are stuffing it back down, your body and emotions will react to it in certain ways. The more unprocessed memories you have, the more they will go somewhere.

Just because you process through an experience, doesn't mean it *goes away* from your mind. You have closets of memories that are stored. When you open the boxes, sort through them, and discard what doesn't serve you, you'll find yourself feeling freer. You can choose what not to focus on when it comes to memories.

Let's say for example you have a damaging past relationship. If you hold every memento, letter, card, gift, and item that represents that relationship, the memories remain more vivid in your mind. If you *clean house*, you will find those memories become much easier to deal with and release.

When I talk about healing past memories, that is much what I'm referring to. You can't erase every memory you hold from your past, but you can deal with the emotional impact it has on you. The more you drudge up that old box, look at all those old letters, and let yourself relive the moment, you'll find the emotions growing—stronger—rather than more faded.

Have you ever talked to someone, and they bring up a past memory which clearly still holds pain? This is often because the emotion has been relived over and over through pulling out that specific memory and reliving it again. The more they talk about that moment in time, the more the emotion will build surrounding it.

Often when people relive a painful memory they will attract more moments similar, because they are currently stuck in that field of thought. The more expectation people have about a subject or situation, they will draw to themselves the same thing.

This is why I want to help you release the past memories, because the more you can open the box, sort through it, and allow your emotions room to heal and breathe, you'll find your life situations altering for the good.

Air out those old memories. Allow them to heal and breathe. After you've dealt with the memory, store it, and allow it to rest. It doesn't mean it goes away completely, but that experience can bring you something valuable in the end.

Affirmation

I air out my memories, and I allow my emotions room to breathe.

Chapter 11: Toxic Memories

Many memories are straight up toxic for you to dwell on. As we talked about in the previous chapter, you can't erase your memories completely, but you can air them out, so that your heart can heal. This can come in many forms for people. You may need to vent, do some emotional exercises, or write some things down.

The key to remember is this—the more you dwell on a toxic memory—the more momentum or power you give to it. For example: if you allow someone who harmed you power through your memories, you will have a harder time truly walking free of the pain.

Memories only have power if you allow them to. This isn't to say certain situations are easy to control such as PTSD or another form of repressed memories. One of the main reasons why people relive toxic memories is that the emotion behind it is unresolved. The soul *wants* to heal it, so it will bring it to the surface through dreams, flashes, people, or other situations.

The energy of a toxic memory needs to be cleaned up. One of the only ways to do that is to allow it to be heard. Once it's heard, you can start to move forward. If you find the memories resurfacing with stronger and stronger emotions, you aren't fully tapping into allowing that emotion room to breathe.

So many of you are scared to let the full strength of your emotions out. Feelings come in layers. You may first have numbness about something—followed by sadness—or anger. The more you allow each emotion about the toxic memory room to breathe, you'll find it dissipating.

Once you've dealt with that emotion, allow the next emotion permission to surface. It may seem you've been dealing with the same memory over and over, but it's not just the memory you're dealing with, it's the layers of emotion buried beneath it.

I want to encourage you to keep un-layering the memory. The more you do, the more freedom you'll feel. Sometimes memories are grouped together, and it's okay to allow several to pop up and heal at the same time. Restructuring your memories takes patience and time with yourself. It's okay to walk one step at a time.

Deal with memories as they come

Sometimes you guys like to go looking for trouble. Instead of allowing your memories to surface and be healed over time, you go rooting around trying to open far too many boxes before you're equipped to handle the energy of all of that.

Allow each toxic memory to be healed at its own pace. Similar to decluttering a house, you wouldn't dump out every piece of content on the floor—it would be far too overwhelming to deal with. Instead, you go through one spot at a time—clearing out what no longer functions for you and moving onto the next project.

You can do this. I promise.

Affirmation

I release toxic memories.

Chapter 12: Replacement Therapy

This is a unique spin on some healing, so I want you to open your heart wide to my words. Although, you can't erase the memories inside your mental home, you can replace them. Let me break this down in some really easy terms for you.

If you have a particular bothersome memory that you've been dealing with for years, you can do an exercise that will help you ease it into something brand new.

Let's say you have a memory at four-years-old that was traumatizing. When you peer into that box, start to see it as you want to see it. For example: let's say you didn't feel safe, and someone hurt you at that age. Instead of repeating that toxic memory and living in distress and fear, replace it with a new memory. See that person how they *should* have treated you. See us angels swooping in and helping that person treat you better and love you the way you deserved to be loved.

You don't have to be alone with that person in the new memory but replace their actions with different actions. It can help ease the transition of the memory from toxic to healthy. There is no time nor space in the mind, and when you replace the memory with a much better one, your mind automatically changes it.

Ask us angels to aid you with these replacements, because they can be painful to deal with. If you truly can't see that person treating you better, replace them with someone you know who *would* treat you better—whether that's one of us angels, Jesus, God, Mother God, or someone you know and trust. See the young version of yourself being cared for and nourished in a beautiful way.

The more you do this—the more you'll find those toxic memories fading quickly away. In the studies of the mind and the quantum field, there is no time. This is why people often revert back to certain ages when something triggers them. That part of their mind is still stuck in a toxic memory, so the more you deal with those memories, the healthier you will respond to situations as an adult.

Whoever you are comfortable with inviting into that memory—do that. If a moment in time pops up into your mind, feel free to ask, *what should have happened? How should they have treated me? I invite (whoever you feel you want to invite) to show me the truth about this situation. Show me love here.* Then allow a new memory to surface and replace the old one.

There may be emotion that pours out, and that's a good sign. Remember to have patience with yourself. You may have to dwell on the new memory you created several times before all of the emotion is released properly.

Affirmation

I lovingly see my memories being replaced.

Chapter 13: Replacing Time

Time is such a fickle thing to us angels. We find it quite funny how you all get caught up in *time*. If you could look at life from a higher plane, you would also crack a smile at the absurdity called *time* that you obsess over.

Time doesn't exist. Your physical plane has these so-called *time* restrictions, because that is how your world was set up, but time—in our world—doesn't exist. This is how you can dabble into the world of the spiritual and see many new things. Such as: future events that transpire, or even stranger—past events you can change.

When you think about your memories, and you attach a time label to them, you'll find it much harder to cope. Instead, looking at time as a blob, or something that's happening simultaneously, you can alter time at any moment.

Let me break this down for you in a little simpler way. If you think you don't revert to childhood—think again. Moment by moment you are working out childhood traumas, beliefs, and structures you created. A child is an open vessel. Time, memories, and situations are placed inside the soul of a child, so that they absorb it and create their reality.

Time is not evil. It's a thought process. When you want to overcome a past memory, pull it into your present moment. Look at it with a higher perspective. Often, you can see the flaws of what happened to you through the eyes of awareness, but the perception of the child within still may see it as truth.

Here's where you take the hand of the inner child and rewrite the time between you two. You can close the gap of *time* in a very short moment. It's acknowledging the child's belief, emotion, and situation—while staying in the now moment.

Have you ever watched yourself throw a tantrum, yet felt completely calm inside? This is the two sides of yourself. The tantrum throwing side needs to be acknowledged, because it wants the bridge to be pulled together with the present moment. The more you let the child-side of yourself control the show, you'll have a harder time understanding how to heal and restore that side.

You are a natural nurturer. You were built to nurture, love, and accept yourself, but often you were taught not to tap into that side. Instead, others may have taught you to deny the emotion, shamed you, or tried to strip away your personal power. It's time to give it all back to yourself.

Nurturing can be taught. If it doesn't come natural for you, start with simple things. Let yourself rest more. Hug longer. Eat healthier. Journal your feelings. Let your inner child feel acknowledged.

Affirmation

I surpass time. I can heal any memory.

Chapter 14: Absorbing the Lessons

The soul is always expanding. Every breath you breathe brings you a new perspective on life. Beneath the pain of a memory is a valuable lesson you can draw on. Many times, these situations look meaningless, but if you look deeper, you'll find you can absorb what's been shown to you.

For example: when someone is abusive toward you, what can you draw from that situation? It may seem like it's only evil, but underneath you can see a shimmer of love. What do I mean by that? The soul who harmed you is lacking love, and you were their source. The lesson you can draw from it is a simple one. *My abuser was powerless and wanted to absorb my love, but this is impossible for anyone, so they never learned their lesson. I can now learn the lesson of love from this, and realize my abuser took out their lack of love on me. It had nothing to do with me.*

Every soul who harms another will only recycle back into a similar lesson. An abuser only takes love, but doesn't give any, so until they learn their source, they will only go through the same thing. The karma of lack of love is a painful one. Your lesson to glean is to find love within yourself to forgive your abuser for not connecting to their source, but rather trying to steal your source of love.

There are levels to souls. Some are on a higher plane, while others are like the abuser—a very low level. A child has a very high-level of pure love, and this is why low-level souls try to steal their source of love. Your job is to release that low-level soul to learn their own lesson.

You may have been an opportunity for them to reflect on their lack of love, yet they refused to grow at that point. I am sorry for your suffering, little ones, and I know it is painful to find the love in these types of situations. Yet, if you do not find the love in the situation, sometimes the one abused will fall into the same low-level state of trying to steal love from another. This isn't always the case, however, you may draw love from others in an unhealthy way due to the abusive *teaching* of someone.

The levels of love

Like we brushed on, there are levels of love. Some souls have not learned how to receive nor give love in a proper way, and this is their life lesson on the physical plane. When you go back into the non-physical you feel the source of love 100%, but the soul doesn't always understand how to operate on the physical level. This is why you learn lessons to teach your soul how to do this.

Whenever you have low-feeling emotions, you can ask yourself, *where am I not connected to my source of love?*

You need love. Every. Single. Day.

In every level there is love. It's up to you to find it. Putting on the mind that love exists in every situation will help you learn the lesson, heal, and move forward from it. If you need support, call on your angels to help you see the love within the problem.

When negative situations exist, often people look at the lack of love. If you put on the eyes of love, you'll start to uncover new depths to everything. Instead of fearing, blaming, or hiding from what's happened throughout your life, you'll embrace it, and search out how you can respond to it by filling it with love.

Love will help your soul absorb the lesson. Without it, the soul repeats the same thing, until it can uncover the source it truly needs. This is similar to how the body will crave energy from food. You may be feeding yourself a very unhealthy diet, so your body is craving food—all the time. The problem is, it's not getting actual *food* from what you're feeding it. Nutrients in earth-grown food feed the body what it needs—while the others are simply fillers.

This is much how lessons and love operate. You can fill the situation with many things: sex, alcohol, shopping, drugs, friends, family, jobs, hobbies, or whatever you think will be a *filler* for your emotional needs, but the true source will always call to you. Love won't stop trying to fill you, and you won't stop wanting it to fill you. In order to absorb the lessons and heal the painful situations from the past, find love within it. No matter how painful—find love.

Affirmation

I receive my lessons through love.

Chapter 15: How to Find Love

Here is the big question I know you're all asking. It's one thing to tell you to *find love* in the lesson, but another to know what to do. Deep within you is the know-how. It is a natural state of being to forgive, love, and hold space for things to heal on their own. The problem us angels see is that you don't remember this part of yourself. You think love is an outside source that needs to get in. When in all reality, it is an inside source that flows out.

People do give love to one another, but it is not your main source. If it becomes your main source you will become very disheartened, because that source won't fill you completely. Similar to what I said about a diet, it may satisfy you to a degree, but it won't stick.

The soul naturally will repel anyone who tries to *suck their source* of love from them. It's not a pleasant feeling. I'm sure many of you have had relationships that felt draining. Why do they feel draining? Because they are trying to attach a hose to your love and take it as their own. That doesn't work. It can sustain a person for a period of time if you don't put an end to it. The more someone sucks your source of love, the more you will feel the low-level emotions toward them.

Love is the highest level of emotion you can feel and attached to it are all kinds of good-feelings for you. If someone is hooked up to your tank of love, and you allow them to drain you, all that will be left is the lower-vibrations.

Set up boundaries

If all you feel is low-level emotions when you're sharing space with someone in whatever form, it's time to set up proper boundaries. Whether they are a child, parent, spouse, friend, co-worker, boss, or anyone at all, your space is your place. When you invite someone into your sacred space, you are giving them permission to share your energy with you. If that person is lacking in love, they may try to infiltrate your love tank and continuously pump it from you.

If you know your limits with someone, you can set up proper boundaries such as: *"No thanks, I can't come to your house today."* You don't need any other excuses, and if they demand one from you, simply repeat your statement. You are never responsible for pleasing someone to make them feel better. I know it may seem selfish, but when you fall into this trap, it's easy to become a love source for multiple people.

Find gratefulness

It's not always easy to find something to be thankful for that was painful. Doing so takes courage, and at times a very creative perspective. When you're met with pain, you can't always see the good in it just yet, but if you continue to look for it, the good will find you on its own.

If your job is falling apart, there's not enough money, or it's stressful, what can you find in it to be grateful for?

- steady income
- the hours
- helps pay some bills

Even if the negative is 75% can you look for the 25% that isn't? This helps you find love in the middle of pain, and in doing so brings healing. In order to bring healing to painful, past memories, find something—anything to be grateful for. Whether it's simply, *they taught me how not to behave with a child.*

In doing so, you are now a better parent. You can understand love in a whole new dimension. You can make the change now.

Wake up each morning and find something to be grateful for. Your bed. Pillow. The sunshine. Your morning coffee. Whatever it is, it'll bring a good-feeling vibe into your day.

If a negative emotion hits you, can you find something in that thought, memory, or emotion to be grateful for?

Happy memories

When you are working on forgiving someone, it may bring up a string of unpleasant memories. One of the best ways to heal from this is to find a happy memory. This doesn't have to be about that specific person or situation, but when you replace the memory with a pleasant one, your brain is triggered to automatically think better thoughts when you feel bad.

Your brain is like a computer, and when you start rewriting its code, it'll go on autopilot to find a better thought when you're feeling negative.

Affirmation

I hold space for love. I give my heart compassion.

Chapter 16: Live in the Moment

One of the best things, and sometimes the hardest to train yourself in, is living in the moment. The mind likes to control situations, and it likes to know what, when, how, and why. What it will do is go back in time and scrape together all the memories it can to protect you. It's not trying to be a bully, but an aid for you.

According to your belief system it will react. If you had a troubled childhood, the brain will infest you with multiple memories that are 'protect mode', which may not always be healthy. For example: if you were raised with an unhealthy father, your brain will put up barriers to keep you safe from those situations (even though it's in the past). Yet, the soul will draw to you what you believe until it is healed or changed.

You can never win with logic

Have you ever been in love? Was logic involved? Emotions fight logic, and they often win. If someone suppresses their emotion about a situation, and uses only logic, eventually the emotion will surface in other ways. This usually involves physical ailments, outbursts, or mental health issues. Emotions cannot be ignored and are tied to memories.

Healing from memories is letting these emotions surface, flow, and be heard.

You can try to "reason" with your emotions, and you may even find yourself saying, *"Why do I keep going back to that? Why do I not listen to myself?"* Are you allowing your emotion to be heard, felt, and loved, or are you smothering your emotion by logic?

I'm sure many of you at one point have tried to help a friend logically with a relationship problem. You may have poured out the best advice on the planet, only to have them do everything opposite of what you told them to do. Why is that? Emotion trumps logic every time.

You are a *feeling* being, and even those who seem to operate without feeling—have deep repressed emotions that they function out of. Their illogical responses seem crazy, and this is because it is crazy. The emotions tied to their actions are not heard, felt, or acknowledged, so it acts out in an irrational way.

The more someone feeds the dysfunctional memory, emotion, and goes back in time, it'll continue the same pattern. Only when you make a choice to find love, be grateful, and work on the memories, do they heal.

Use love as your bouncing board

If you often use people as your bouncing board such as: *everyone betrays me, hurts me, and isn't loyal to me*, you'll find the painful memories continuing. This is often because your mind, heart, and soul doesn't see the opposite right now. You may have beautiful friendships, family, and relationships in your life, but because of your pain you'll only experience the opposite. Even if someone is kind to you, and your memory is left unhealed, you may think, *what do they want from me? Why are they being so nice?*

This kind of mistrust breeds more mistrust and will collapse any solid relationship that's in your life.

Living beyond yesterday

It's no easy feat to come out of past memories and live in today, but in order to truly change your life you must embrace *today.* The perfecting of today and tomorrow is what you decide to do with it. If you go backward and rehash what people have done, those people have control over your today and tomorrow. If you embrace the now moment, you'll find peace, love, joy, and happiness is sitting there waiting for you to embrace them.

Letting the memories be just that—memories—will bring peace to your mind. You're not in that moment anymore, and now you can embrace your much better life. Even if today feels turbulent, find something in it that brings love.

Sifting through the noise

Every day you are bombarded with noise from the outside. You see it in the form of relationships, social media, television, work, health, and anything else that occupies your brain space.

Pull yourself back to center. Whenever things get too cluttered or noisy, it'll be harder to truly live in the present moment. Have you ever had a huge project that felt impossible to tackle? What happened when you concentrated on everything at the same time?

Noise.

Try refocusing onto one solid thing and letting yourself work on the first step. Now what happened? It's much easier to cope and get things accomplished when you pull back from the chaos of everything else. If your mind is busy thinking of so and so's problem, this work issue, your spouse's bad attitude, or all the tasks you have to accomplish—it creates far too much chaos in your mind.

Past memories are very much the same. How can you enjoy the present with the people in your life, if the past memories are bringing noise and chaos everywhere you go? It would be like trying to have a one-on-one conversation with someone, and fifteen other people were yelling for your attention. Soon, you wouldn't be able to hear that individual at all.

Many want to tackle the multiple problems they think they have in their life, but here's where it all falls apart. Your soul understands what you can handle, and if you tackle too much at once, you'll simply shut down. Healing past memories takes time. Support yourself through it. One step at a time.

Affirmation

I embrace today.

Chapter 17: Awakening the Healer Within

Every one of you has a healer within. Your natural state is wholeness, health, and vitality. When you fall into a state of disarray, the body naturally tries to warn you of the discord. This is why people develop 'dis-ease', anxiety, depression, or a form of discomfort on this physical plane. The natural level co-exists with the spiritual and emotional levels.

The body releases exactly what you need when you need it—when you are existing peacefully within yourself. The body has the right chemicals at the right time to bring you ease, comfort, and peace. The problem is many do not allow the flushing of negative emotions from their system. Instead, they hoard them up, until dis-ease finds them, and suddenly they become aware of what's going on. (Most the time.) The body gives off warning signals.

Have you ever felt a subtle warning or piece of advice that you ignored? Your body may have whispered to you, *stop eating that, drink more water, go outside...* When you do not heed the body's voice there may be negative side effects as a result. Such as obesity, dehydration, aches and pains, stress...

Ask your body questions

Your body will give you impulses. Have you ever been going about your day, when you get a sensation to grab something, say something, or write something down? Your body's intelligence is giving you warning to help you stay at ease later on in the day. How many of you have chastised yourself when you didn't listen to that information you received?

Your body sends messages to you, because it is keen on keeping you healthy, happy, and alive. It's a primal part of you that is important. When you feel upset, tired, hungry, stressed, angry, sad, or emotional in any way, that is the body's warnings to help you come back into balance. If it seems you wrestle with negative feelings more than accepting the positive ones, again they are warnings to help you.

The body leads you toward healing

The body's *natural* state is to lead you toward health. When you get into a vicious cycle such as addiction—the body's natural system is being thwarted. Buried beneath the noise is its voice to help you stay in perfect health.

You are naturally drawn to good things such as—peace, love, joy, and healing, but when the body becomes addicted to drama, it can create a whole world of problems.

How many have said or heard, *I hate drama!* This is because it is the body, soul, and spirit's wisdom that is speaking through this. The body doesn't like drama, because it throws it into a state of chaos—same as the soul and spirit.

The addiction of the body and mind can keep you in a perpetual state of craving excitement, drama, and new things. The way the world is built is to keep people's attention, which includes the next best thing, drama, and exciting stories. TV, news, and social media are all grabbing for your attention. How do they do that? *Drama*. It may not all be bad drama, but it's drama nonetheless. This thrusts each and every one of you into daily choices to walk in peace or follow the chaos.

Drama leads to more drama

Just like any addiction, you'll need *more* drama to pacify your needs. When you understand that drama is a literal chemical addiction, you can realize why you crave getting on social media to argue or binge watching a dramatic show.

Keep these things in mind when it comes to your healing. Being addicted to past drama can also create future drama in your life. The more you dwell on past experiences, the more they filter into your every day life.

Attention

You have our undivided attention each day. Most human souls crave drama, because they crave attention on them. Sympathy, empathy, love, and compassion are emotions you may desire for someone to give you. Turn your attention on yourself, ask for help, and you will hear incredible wisdom.

Many call this stream of wisdom *God, higher-self, Holy Spirit, angels,* or something altogether different. Wisdom is naturally built inside of you. Your state of being is healing, peace, wellness, and life.

Affirmation

I ask my body questions and let it lead me to healing.

Chapter 18: Being Gentle

Be gentle on yourself. Often you want to leap before you're ready to heal. You must be in-sync with what you want before starting the journey of past memory healing.

There are levels to healing, belief, and your journey through life. If you're trying to get to level 5 before you've grown to reach the ladder of level 3, you will only walk away feeling bad, disappointed, angry, hurt, or depressed about your life. You must take small increments forward to get you onto the next level of belief.

Have you heard yourself or others say, *I can't do that. I've never been able to do that.* If you stay on that level, you'll only be able to see, hear, and experience that particular level. Have you met others who have an opposing view as you? Even when you present them with different scenarios, sides, and information, they still refuse to see? Why do you think that is?

When you are only able to handle the level you're on, and you're not ready for the next, you will simply refuse the information that could help you grow to reach the next step. You may look at level 5 and feel pain that you're not able to have it, because level 5 is not what you can handle just yet. If you take a step back, go to level 2, and then focus on level 3...you'll find your steps much easier.

You've heard the term—baby steps, right? When a child is learning to walk, they don't automatically have sturdy legs. They wobble. Even long after a child learns to walk, they still wobble.

When you're learning a baby step at a time, expect yourself to falter, fail, or fall down. That's how everyone learns. Experience can come through disappointment, regret, fear, or other not good feeling emotions. It's what you do with those emotions that counts. Can you learn to accept the wobble in your life, take the hand of someone perhaps a bit sturdier, and move forward?

Children observe their elders. They constantly try to mimic those around them. When you're in the learning stages within any subject, you'll find yourself trying to mimic people who've gone before you. This is perfectly okay, but also remember you have your own personal path of learning.

When you're learning a new subject (or an old subject in a brand-new way) you'll come across bumps. When you find yourself feeling bad, take a step back and ask yourself, *am I trying to jump a step before I'm ready?*

Let go of trying to be where someone else is currently at

It's okay to observe them but accepting where you are and moving forward at your pace is vital. Every child learns at a different pace. If you have children you understand this. Pushing a child beyond where they are willing only leads to more frustration.

Take potty training for example. Many children will show signs they are ready to embark on this journey, while others will stand in resistance. If you force a child to potty train what happens? If you ask most parents, they will tell you that it took much longer when they tried to make their kid do it. When kids were ready it became *easy.*

Your baby steps will feel light, easy, and joyful. If you find resistance in something—go back and move a bit slower.

Not that there won't be resistance in things you're trying to improve, but you'll find it much easier when you focus in on the baby steps—instead of a giant leap forward.

How does a baby learn?

If you watch a child you'll notice they repeat. The more they repeat something, the deeper it goes into their subconscious brain. At this early stage all they do is absorb what's shown them.

Whatever you repeat will become a part of you. Here's the real fun part. You can change what's around you by refocusing. Whatever habit you have formed, you can un-form. All it takes is one step forward at a time in the right direction. Don't worry so much when it feels you've backpedaled from what you're trying to accomplish. This just requires more gentleness to urge the little child inside to see the truth.

Affirmation

I will be gentle with myself and move at my own pace.

Let's talk about signs for a minute. Signs can be a great tool to get to know yourself, your fears, and what you're ready for. When a sign pops up (an emotion, body pain, past memory, relationship issue, or spiritual sign) you can easily take a step back as the observer and discover the meaning behind the sign.

Be honest with yourself

Discovering what the sign means can take a dose of patience. You may not understand a particular situation or emotion right away, but when you're gentle and observe yourself, it'll soon unlock its secrets.

Us angels love to drop you hints and signs when it comes to your life. We may send you signs of:

- Love
- Support
- Warning

The more you see a particular sign, pay close attention. For example, Z.Z. was seeing blown out tires over and over on the road. She noticed it, but the sign didn't quite register. After a little while, she found herself saying, *is this a sign for me?* When she went and got her car checked out, sure enough the mechanic told her the situation. Her shocks had made her tires dangerous. She immediately got both problems fixed.

This was a warning sign.

You don't want to rely solely on signs throughout your life but be aware of them. When you repeat a relationship pattern, friendship, job, situation, emotion, or see something in a repetitive type manner, look into it further.

Signs are for you to feel supported in all you do. They are actions of the divine that help heal, direct, warn, and encourage you throughout your life. If you do not receive consistent signs, don't fret about it. Sometimes you are simply *missing* the signs that are in front of you—much like how Z.Z. didn't notice the blown-out tires for a while.

If a past memory seems to be surfacing whether through dreams, visions, emotions or anything of the sort, it simply means that memory is ready to be healed. If you keep shoving it aside, (much like a sign) it'll only keep reoccurring in different ways.

Signs may come in many forms. If one doesn't work, another will pop up. Your soul desires healing. It looks for it. Working through things a day at a time will help you see clearer what's in front of you.

- Does your mind race when you wake up?
- Do you have a hard time falling asleep?
- Do people remind you of trauma from the past?

These are also signs to uncover truths. Drastic changes may need to occur for you to bring those painful memories to a head and be able to heal them.

Have you ever had something under the surface of your skin that is painful? It hasn't come to a head yet, but you know it's there. If you try to force it to surface, it only seems to bruise or wound you more. This is how painful memories occur. You may desire to heal it, but it must be able to come to a head, so that you can fully feel supported, healed, and deal with the situation for what it is.

A sign will begin to appear the readier you are to address the painful memory. It's not easy to look at a past memory square in the face—especially one that was traumatic. I'm not here to dredge up old issues, but simply to help you through ones that are surfacing into your current life.

It's not our job to stir up trouble in your soul, but rather help you get through the turmoil that is arising on its own. Each of you possess the intelligence to understand why something is coming up for you. Your soul knows what needs to be healed. This is a common phrase I hear from many of you, *there are too many traumas to deal with. Most of them I don't even know what they are.*

Here's where baby steps come in. Small changes. You don't have to go digging up old past roots all at once. In fact, you don't have to dig them up at all. Memories will surface on their own throughout your life. It's simply our job and yours to uncover why and gently remove those old roots.

One of the quickest ways to pull up an old root is to remind yourself of where you are now. When you remind the soul of all the joyful, thankful, and beautiful things you have, the root will dissolve much quicker in this frame of mind.

Affirmation

Each baby step I take gets me closer to my goals.

Chapter 20: Taking Care of the Inner Child

How do you wish you would have been treated as a child?

When you grow up, you understand a lot more than when you were young. You understand injustice, cruelty, and abuse. You learned to recognize the way you were treated wasn't healthy. Here's the thing that most of you don't quite understand. The inner child doesn't always get it.

Children turn things inward, and the way they develop in the early years can be difficult. Although your adult brain may get what's going on, your inner child may still cling to the false beliefs it was raised with. It's your job, as the nurturer, to fully help the inner child heal.

You may have noticed two sides to yourself. The child and the adult. When the child gets sad, frustrated, overwhelmed, abused, or anything challenging, it will revert back to the way it was raised. The adult generally will look at the behavior of the inner child and may do several things: criticize, bully, or encourage and love. If you were raised with critical people around you, your natural adult instinct will be to bully, push, and force your inner child to do what you want.

- How is that working for you?

It takes time and development for you to train the adult side of you to react correctly to the pain of your child-like self. Every part of you is in the inside. From age zero to adult. Depending on the past trauma or memory, it will trigger a specific age range. If you can learn to recognize that reaction, love the little self, and offer comfort, you'll find yourself overcoming things much quicker.

Not everyone has the natural instincts to care for a child. Us angels have watched the human race for years, and we have seen much nurturing and much neglect. There are streaks in families of unnatural abuse and neglect. We have sent earth angels in the midst of those families to break the mold that's occurred in those generations.

You may feel like you don't understand why *you* were treated so poorly, when your natural instinct is completely opposite of the families before you. This is why. You are an earth angel, here to help that generation change their ways. Let it start with you, little one. Support your inner child.

We are sending many, many earth angels to help with the situation of abuse and neglect. It breaks our heart to see the human race repeating the same patterns. You must take the next step up. Let me break down a few things for you. An earth angel is a term we use, because it represents a human soul who, despite being abused, neglected, or treated poorly…still doesn't let her or his soul grow hard. You still love. You still try.

This is embedded in you from birth, because you've been given a mission to help heal your family line. That doesn't mean your current family will ever change their ways, but YOU can change your family line. Your children and their children can be the deciding factor.

Your family's souls are valuable, but they must learn their own lessons. It's up to you to make those strides forward to heal, change, grow, and move forward. If you're saying to me, *but I don't have kids or a family*, you can still break the negative family line by being different. Every soul you touch right now is family. You are all family.

If you share your story and encourage another person, you are healing your family. Us angels are your family. God is your family. Your neighbor is your family. Everyone around you is connected to you, and if you choose to see it that way, you'll come to understand your deeper purpose in life.

Words are powerful. A single sentence can ring in a soul's mind for their entire life, unless you break the power of those words.

Have you ever been going about your day when suddenly you felt like someone was discussing you? It's simply a sensation, which can lead to positive or negative emotions. I want to teach you a few things to help something like this. The words could be from a past memory, or they could be a current situation.

Look at the words for what they are—energy. Energy can be altered. You can turn the negative energy around for your good. Can you learn from the past experience?

Lessons are scattered throughout your life, and it's up to you to unlock the door of their meaning. Abuse or neglect may not seem to have a lesson buried in it, but it does. Simply look at the soul who harmed you, and come to understand that their level of love is little. It had nothing to do with you specifically. No matter who would have been in their path—they would have abused. This takes the pressure off your individual soul. If you can learn the lesson in that, it'll help release the painful memory much easier.

Every soul has a path. Each path is peppered with choices for that person. When they choose poorly they impact other souls around them (who also have a choice to how they react to the lesson).

Children don't have the development quite yet to pick and choose lessons from their experiences. They simply take it all personal. This is why I'm here to support your inner child understand the pain in the memory, so that the memory can be healed.

Affirmation

I choose to love.

Thank you for reading:

How to Heal Past Memories with Archangel Zadkiel

Visit: eepurl.com/cV-Trf for your

FREE

GIFT

Angel Guidance for Wealth

If you've enjoyed this book, I would love for you to post a review. As an author, I am always learning and growing, and I'd love to hear back from you.

Come visit me on:

Facebook: Z.Z.'s Angel Card Corner

Instagram: @Z.Z. Rae

Blog: www.angelguidancetoday.wordpress.com

Facebook Group: Empath Connection

Website: www.zzrae.com

Printed in Great Britain
by Amazon

17116738R00071